TABLE OF CONTENTS

INTRODUCTION

Why a book on forgiveness? Road rage, rampant divorce, and schoolyard shootings dramatically demonstrate the need for reconciliation and healing of relationships in today's world.

The Power of Forgiving will help you come to an understanding of why forgiveness is the only way to arrive at complete healing from the hurts caused by others. It gives you practical advice on how to approach others whom you have hurt or who have hurt you.

It's all here in the stories of people just like you...the agony, the pain, the problems, the inner torture, the plotting of revenge against those who have devastated your life...and the answers that will bring peace back into your life. Although it's a quick read, this book may not be an easy read because you cannot read it without doing some serious thinking. I challenge you to use it as a time to be honest with yourself.

The Power of Forgiving is a practical, down-to-earth, where-the-rubber-meets-the-road kind of book. Take it along with you in your purse or pocket. Read and meditate on a chapter at a time. Perhaps you might send a copy to someone you know...but let the book speak into their life.

Much of this material has appeared first as sermons for congregations I have served over the years. I am grateful to many who have contributed to these concepts...most are unidentifiable. Whenever possible, credit has been given. My thanks also to the many folks who have shown me in real life how to forgive and be forgiven.

My prayer for you is that this book will have a positive impact on you and the people you know.

—*Robert J. Strand*
Springfield, Missouri 2000

DEDICATION

This book is dedicated to my son, Kent,
who was paralyzed in an auto accident
at age five and has every reason to be bitter,
but instead has lived a life of forgiveness.

Chapter 1

I'LL NEVER FORGIVE!

"This is it! I've had it! I'm calling it quits with her!" Shouting to the barren, sagebrush covered, dry land surrounding him, the lean, weathered man resolutely stood up from his rocky seat and began making his way down from the mesa to their ranch house below. He would put an end to this whole night—no, this whole decade—of wrestling with frustration, with silence, with anger. Now...he would take his revenge. Resolve hardened in his heart.

Looking back...it had all begun so wonderfully. There had been the courtship and honeymoon followed by their first years of working hard together to make the ranch a success, and then their shared excitement when the kids had been born. The ranch was now doing great. Life had been good in those beginning years.

Then...there was that first night 10 years ago when she wouldn't talk. It was strange, that silence. The kids chattered over the supper and she smiled. But he knew something, something gray and sinister

1

had come between them. He was puzzled. This strange silent behavior stretched on for months. Years passed…it was a strange, silent coexistence which, in time, made their oldest son so embittered that he eventually ran away. The younger ones were also negatively affected.

She soon found a liquid solution…vodka. There were times in the last few years when it seemed as though the alcohol made things a bit better—she would at least talk. Last night, when once again she had too much to drink, she began talking and it all spilled out. She recalled their happiness of past days. Then she seemed to hit a wall…she froze, her voice trailing off.

He encouraged her…and out it came. A man had been stopping by the ranch when she was alone. For her it was a break in the long days…for him it had been much more. She had laughed off his advances at first…but in a moment of passion yielded once, then again and again. Ten years of this festering guilt, pain, and fear of discovery surfaced. At the end of her story, she defiantly said, "I won't tell you who it is, and you'll never guess!"

He demanded that she tell him the man's identity as anger, hatred, and revenge began to churn inside him. For 10 years he'd accepted it all without protesting; now, his worst fears were confirmed. Anger consumed him as he pressured her to tell him. Finally she confessed that it was his best friend.

He was stunned! The one man whom he'd

trusted the most. Something soured and died inside him and made his blood turn cold. "I'll get him for this!" he told himself over and over again. He made his plans with cold calculation. "I'll start by telling his wife, and she'll make his life miserable. I'll rub his face in the dirt until he's destroyed…then, I'll shoot him, not to kill, but to disable him enough to make sure he'll never be the same again."

All that lonely night he had wandered over the brushy mesa…at times, hot with rage, then cold with icy hatred. Morning now had finally come.

When he got back to the house, he realized it was Sunday, and the kids were all ready to go to church.

Later he would say, "Why I went to church that morning, I'll never know. Something deep in my soul must have been crying for help."

Dropping the kids at the entrance, he parked the car and slowly made his way into the little country church. Inside the door, there the man stood—his best friend—hand outstretched in greeting!

He describes his moment of decision: "My hand froze in my pocket…the struggle was almost too much. I had promised to take revenge upon him. I had vowed to make him pay! But all of a sudden, my red hot hatred fought with the truth—God's truth—that broke over me as I faced my enemy. It was the truth that I had repeated hundreds of times in and out of church: 'Forgive us our debts, as we also have forgiven our debtors…' (Matthew 6:12). Then…more truth: 'But if you do not forgive men their sins, your Father will not forgive your sins'" (Matthew 6:15).

3

The moment seemed frozen in time.

"With a sob in my soul, my hand became un-frozen and reached out to grip his. I took the hand of the man who had betrayed everything I loved. For the first time in my life, I knew what it was to forgive. It was a moment of release…a release to all the pent up bitterness and anger of 10 years. I was finally free to live again!"

He took the next step when he got home that day. Shutting their bedroom door to the bustle of Sunday dinner, he took her hands in his and said, "I forgive you. I accept you just like I did on that day when we pledged to love and to cherish each other until death do us part."

Then the healing began its slow progress.

FORGIVENESS IS OUTRAGEOUSLY COSTLY!

(Matthew 6:12,15)

POWER POINT: Is there someone in your life who has severely offended you—someone whom you've never forgiven? As you begin to read this book, ask God to help you find forgiveness for this person.

Chapter 2

WHAT IS FORGIVENESS?

Whatever it is...there is a desperate hunger for it! In Spain, there is a father and his teenage son whose relationship became so strained that the son ran away from home. His father, however, soon began to search for his rebellious, wayward son. Finally, after having exhausted all the possibilities, he made one last desperate effort to find his son. The father placed an ad in the Madrid newspaper. The ad read: "Dear Paco, meet me in front of the newspaper office at noon. All is forgiven. I love you. Please come home. Your father."

The next day, at noon, in front of the newspaper 800 "Pacos" showed up...each one seeking forgiveness and love from his father.[1]

So...what is "forgiveness"? Normally we tend to think of it in one or more of the following terms: to pardon, excuse, cease to feel resentment against, remit the penalty of, acquit, set free, wipe the slate clean, or let bygones be bygones. So it's something we understand quite easily; we know the meaning; we know how it works; and, above all, we want others to forgive us when we have wronged them. Just because we know what it is doesn't make it any easier to do ourselves.

Let's look at it from other perspectives:

FORGIVENESS IS LIKE...

The wind-blown bud which blooms in placid beauty on the WWI battlefield at Verdun.

The tiny slate-gray sparrow which has built its nest of twigs and string among the shards of glass upon the crumbled wall that divided a city.

The child who laughs in merry ecstasy beneath the toothed fence that encloses DaNang.

The fragrance of the violet that still clings fast to the heel that crushed it.

The reed that stands up straight and green when nature's mighty rampaging tornado halts, fully spent.

FORGIVENESS IS...

The disabled veteran who returns as an ambassador of goodwill, to help rebuild a ravaged country, to give something to 'Nam.

The father, with arms wide open, who welcomes the prodigal son or daughter back home with celebration.

The Son hanging on a cross, soon to take a last breath, who says, "Father forgive them for they know not what they do."

Forgiveness is a God who will not leave us nor forsake us after all we've done!

Yes…it's an easily understood concept. But most of us stall out when we ask the question, "Why?" Okay, good question. Why should we forgive? In fact, why should anyone forgive? Why shouldn't the person who has committed the wrong be made to pay for the sin? It's such a natural way of thinking: "Somebody's got to pay!"

Forgiveness seems too easy a way out for the one who wronged us. There really should be an eye for an eye and a tooth for a tooth—the Old Testament tells us that. We want to take it even further…slur for slur, slam for slam, blood for blood. But who will be the referee? Who will decide that your return hit equaled the one you were given? How many Serbs will be killed to atone for the Bosnians who were slain? Where does this circle of revenge end? There's an old saying:

> Doing an injury puts you below your enemy; revenging an injury makes you but even with him; forgiving sets you above him.

Revenge is a poor weapon because it lowers you to your enemy's level. And, what's worse, it boomerangs. The person who seeks revenge is like the person who shoots himself in order to hit the enemy with the kick of the gun's recoil. Revenge is the most worthless weapon in the world! It ruins the avenger while more firmly enabling the enemy to stay an enemy. It initiates an endless flight down the bottomless stairway of rancor, anger, reprisals, bitterness, ruthless retaliation, law-suits, and frustration. Repayment is impossible, and revenge is impotent.

Therefore, the only way out is to do the right thing, the thing you know must be done…to forgive!

(Luke 23:34)

⚡ POWER POINT: Have you ever taken verbal revenge on someone, then later regretted it? Call to mind those whom you've treated this way during the last month and resolve to ask their forgiveness.

[1]From a bulletin at the Billy Graham Crusade in Southern California.

Chapter 3

I'D RATHER HATE MY ENEMY!

What? No repayment? No revenge? Then I will enjoy the satisfaction of hating the dirty rascal! Well, yes, you can hate your enemy. It's a choice. You can hate him; you can nurse a grudge until it has become a full-blown hate...hooves, horns, tail, fire-breathing, and all.

But again, what will you gain? In hatred, as in taking revenge, everybody loses. To hold onto hate will cause you to become a different person. Hate will turn a likable woman into a disagreeable complainer. Hate can turn a warm, wonderful man into a caustic cynic. Hate will divide a community down the middle. Hate can even cause a doctor to lose patients. Two doctors who shared a small office building in Texas had a feud going. One doctor eventually accused the other one of hiring a hit man to kill him. A divider was placed in the waiting area to partition it in half. What effect do you think this had on their patients? You can bet that after one trip to the divided office, a number of them decided to look elsewhere for medical care. Counselors will lose clients; salespeople will lose sales—both advice and sales many times depend on developing relationships. And a preacher given to hatred will lose church members, for it is almost impossible to effectively minister to others out of a bitter spirit. To hate is a lose-lose situation.

What will it cost you to continue to incubate your hatred? Plenty! What does the Bible have to say?

> *The acts of the sinful nature are obvious: sexual immorality, impurity and debauchery; idolatry and witchcraft; hatred, discord, jealousy, fits of rage, selfish ambitions, dissensions, factions and envy...I warn you, as I did before, that those who live like this will not inherit the kingdom of God* (Galatians 5:19-21).

Hatred will cost you dearly...here as well as in the life to come. Dr. William Sadler writes:

> No one can appreciate so fully as a doctor the amazingly large percentage of human disease and suffering which is directly traceable to worry, fear, and hate. The sincere acceptance of the principles and teachings of Christ with respect to the life of mental peace and joy...would at once wipe out more than half the difficulties, diseases, and sorrows of the human race.

In other words, the teachings of Jesus, when applied to our modern civilization, would so revitalize us that the present human race would immediately stand out as a special order of beings. Living the Christ-life will pay huge dividends just for the mental and moral rewards it affords here in this present life, let alone in the world to come.

Shakespeare knew enough of the Bible and perhaps a bit of psychiatry to recognize that people can become sick from hatred and unconfessed or covered sin. He painted a vivid picture of such psychosomatic overtones in Lady Macbeth. When Macbeth asked the doctor about her illness, he replied:

> Not so sick, my lord,
> As she is troubled with thick-coming fancies,
> That keep her from her rest.
> (Macbeth, v.3,38)

Shakespeare's good doctor was then asked much the same question put to many of our present day physicians:

> Canst thou not minister to mind diseas'd,
> Pluck from the memory a rooted sorrow,
> Raze out the written troubles of the brain,
> And with some sweet oblivious antidote
> Cleanse the stuff'd bosom of that perilous stuff
> Which weighs upon the heart?
> (Macbeth, v.3,40)

The problem is that when any of us hates another, we become enslaved to that person! There is no way to escape the tyrannical grasp of hate on the mind. Work can no longer be enjoyed because even there the person we hate is ever in our thoughts.

Vacations cause little pleasure because the person we hate will vacation with us, in our mind. The simple joys in life, such as driving a new car, are marred; you might just as well be driving a buckboard in the rain.

King Solomon must have had much the same kind of an experience because he once wrote: "Better a meal of vegetables where there is love than a fattened calf with hatred" (Proverbs 15:17).

The person you hate can physically be hundreds of miles away from you, but thoughts of him or her can still be more cruel than any slave driver. Thoughts of the person you hate can whip you into a frenzy until the soft innerspring mattress you lay down upon at night becomes as uncomfortable as a bed of nails! There is an antidote to hatred:

> *Put to death, therefore, whatever belongs to your earthly nature. But now you must rid yourselves of all such things as these: anger, rage, malice, slander...put on the new self, which is being renewed in knowledge in the image of its Creator. Bear with each other and forgive whatever grievances you may have against one another. Forgive as the Lord forgave you. And over all these virtues put on LOVE, which binds them all together in perfect unity!* (Colossians 3:5, 8,10,13-14)

(Proverbs 15:17)

 POWER POINT: Consider how much unforgiveness has cost you in the last year.

12

Chapter 4

WHAT IF I JUST IGNORE IT?

Repayment seems impossible...revenge is impractical...resentment is too impotent...so what is left? What about some kind of a peaceful coexistence? *I won't hate that person any more. I promise not to hit or hurt that person, not even with my words. I'll just ignore him. Live and let live I say.* How about that? Won't that just handle this little problem? I'll just ignore him or her because they aren't worth the trouble any more.

Not so fast! None of us, including you, can afford the luxury of an unforgiving attitude. However, there could be one exception—if you will never have any need of forgiveness yourself. The problem is that all of us are in need of forgiveness...and often. We need the forgiveness of our fellow humans; and much more seriously, we need the forgiveness of God our heavenly Father. These two concepts go hand in hand.

Jesus said: "For if you forgive men when they sin

against you, your heavenly Father will also forgive you" (Matthew 6:14). Forgiving and being forgiven are all of one piece. They cannot be separated. The person who refuses to forgive cuts himself off from the forgiveness of others as well as forgiveness from the Lord.

General James Oglethorpe once said to John Wesley: "I will never forgive."

"Then I hope, sir," replied Wesley, "you never sin."

The person who loves God must also love a neighbor...in fact, all neighbors. The one who hates a brother cannot love God. Loving God and loving another person are indivisible.

George Herbert put it like this: "He that cannot forgive others breaks the bridge over which he himself must pass if he would ever reach heaven; for everyone has need to be forgiven."

The life that is lived with a sense of being open to the love of God is also a life which is open to loving others. The person who receives forgiveness from God is a person who is also forgiving of others. "Because of the Lord's great love we are not consumed, for his compassions never fail. They are new every morning; great is your faithfulness" (Lamentations 3:22-23). If this is true, and Jesus said it is, then forgiving and being forgiven form the one crucial, central, and eternal matter of every life.

Is this an impossible task? Not for the person who *has been* forgiven by God in the past and *is being* forgiven on a daily basis. Forgiveness allows a person

14

who has been forgiven the opportunity to also forgive. There is a rush of God's strength which empowers us to forgive.

The contrast between our debt to God (which is made by our accumulating sins against His will and His Word) and the debts others may owe us is immeasurable. Nothing that others can do to us will in any way begin to compare with what we have done to God! It's an ongoing process...we daily need the forgiveness of God because we are so human, so frail, so weak, so prone to doing our own thing. And when God has forgiven us the debt we owe Him, how can we be unforgiving to others who owe us so little in comparison?

Anything done to us by others that we may need to forgive is only a shadow of the debt we have been forgiven by God. When we realize the extent of God's forgiveness toward us, we should be easily able to answer the question: Must I forgive others? This answer should be quickly forthcoming from our hearts. Forgive? Yes!

It's at our own peril that we will ignore or gloss over someone who needs our forgiveness! Ignore it? No! Forgive as you have been forgiven!

(Lamentations 3:22-23)

⚡ POWER POINT: Take a few minutes and make a list of all those you can think of who need your forgiveness. Feel the weight lift as you forgive them in your heart!

Chapter 5

THE BEST MEDICINE

"Do you want to be well badly enough to forgive her?" the counselor gently asked.

He just sat there staring into space…seething in hatred, fiery eyes, drawn face, tense, and quivering chin. He didn't deny it, he couldn't deny it…he had plenty of reason to hate, to really hate.

For years his emotionally sick wife had accused him of running around on her. He had suffered more than once from her continual verbal abuse. Yet, he had chosen to stay with her. Why? He didn't know, except that his church taught against divorce, and there were children involved.

Now all the kids were grown and gone…all of them had been scarred from a destructive home environment. He had recently felt the final, brutal, intense blow when he discovered that she had been carrying on an affair with another man for some years. He had immediately filed for divorce!

He's alone, now…chronically depressed, hurting from the pains of the past, brooding over the injustices of life, visiting a counselor in order to put his life back together. He is one bitter man!

Several moments passed before he mustered his thoughts enough to finally respond to the counselor. "Why do I have to forgive her?"

Why, indeed?

Okay...let me give you some answers to that piercing question:

Forgiveness is essential to good health. The emotional pain that too many people are experiencing results from an inability, for whatever reason, to either grant or receive forgiveness. This is one of the most common crippling symptoms of people who are suffering from emotional pain. And emotional pain, nurtured long enough, will eventually result in physical pain. An upset mind equals an upset body.

Unforgiving people are bitter and angry. People who won't grant forgiveness are eventually devastated by their bitterness. Too often they don't see it this way. Their bitterness blinds them to their anger. For many it's easier to say, "I'm hurt" than it is to admit, "I'm angry." If one of these angry people finally gets in touch with their anger, they are likely to justify it as being a necessary defense against being hurt again. This bitterness and anger is their motivation to get even. Further, it prevents them from getting close enough to anyone to be hurt again.

Unforgiving people waste their life's energy. This kind of person tends to harbor resentment and is always on the lookout for the opportunity to take revenge. This person is blinded to the fact that he is being hurt more by an unwillingness to forgive than is the person from whom he is withholding forgiveness. It takes quite a bit of mental energy and resources to keep hurtful memories alive!

The question "Why do I have to forgive him or her?" reveals the mindset that forgiving another is something unfair, something that God has unjustly put upon us poor humans.

In part, it's to spare the Christian this unnecessary drain of life energy that Paul advised: "Get rid of all bitterness, rage and anger, brawling and slander, along with every form of malice. Be kind and compassionate to one another, forgiving each other, just as in Christ God forgave you" (Ephesians 4:31-32).

In an honest act of forgiving, we most often see the person being forgiven as the one who benefits the most. Not so! In reality, just the reverse is true! If you could only take a peek into the client files of most counselors…I know you would find a huge percentage of cases where people continue to be crippled by guilt for things which have been long forgotten by the other party involved.

God himself released His offense at our sins. This sin was so completely absorbed by Christ's death that God the Father is able to say of those who accept His forgiveness: "I will forgive their wickedness and will remember their sins no more" (Jeremiah 31:34).

Forgiving is the only thing that releases us from an unfair past. If you choose not to forgive, you can stick with the unfair past because revenge is about the only recourse left open. And revenge will only keep you glued to your past history. It dooms you to repeat it again and again.

Revenge never works because people keep score differently. How many bombing raids can equal the Holocaust? How many cutting remarks will equal the slap in the face? Forgiving takes us off the elevator of revenge. We can start over again as if the wrong-doer had not done anything to us.

Forgiveness brings release to the forgiver. It's the person who has been hurt who most feels the burden of this unfairness. But unforgiveness only condemns the self to more unfairness. Is it fair to be walloped again and again by the memory of a past that is unjust? Vengeance is having a videotape planted in your soul that cannot be turned off—it plays the painful scene over and over and each time you feel the hurt. Forgiving turns off the videotape of painful memory! Forgiving sets you free. Forgiving is the only way back to health.

Forgiveness is the medicine your heart needs in order to keep you open to God's wonderful possibilities for your future. Nothing...absolutely nothing can erase the hurts of the past and open the opportunities of the future more effectively than a good dose of the medicine of forgiveness!

(Ephesians 4:31-32; Jeremiah 31:34)

POWER POINT: Do you have an illness that may be caused or aggravated by unforgiveness? Is it worth it? Think about how forgiveness can improve your quality of life.

Chapter 6

WHAT NEEDS TO BE FORGIVEN?

No one really forgives until or unless that one has been hurt, deeply hurt, and experienced real pain. We can too easily turn this miracle of forgiveness into nothing more than a cheap indulgence when we go through the motions of forgiving people who have never deeply hurt us. Unless you are hurt...talk of something else.

Not every hurt needs to be forgiven! There are problems which should merely be shrugged off or simply chalked up to the fact that we are human beings.

Consider the following:

Annoyances... There will always be people who annoy you by telling the same old stale stories over and over again or those who cut ahead of you at the checkout line. At one time or another, you'll en-counter folks on the road who tailgate, weave in traffic, become distracted while talking on their cell phones, drive in the wrong lane, and do similar an-noying things.

Defeats... Some people will succeed where you might fail. Some, whom you may consider inferior, will get promoted over you. Then there are the early birds who always seem to get the best of the bargains before you appear on the scene, and those teams which seem to be able to win when yours are defeated.

Slights... People whom we want to impress ignore us when we strive to be noticed. We seem to always be on the outside looking in, never quite making it to that coveted inner circle. Perhaps the boss even fails to invite you to the wedding of his daughter.

Yes, such things do hurt! But let's be real about this, they are not the kinds of actions that need to be forgiven. Such things simply require tolerance, indulgence, magnanimous overlooking, or an application of humility.

The hurts that need forgiving are deep and moral ones—ones that build walls, cut deep into the soul, and slice the fiber which holds our relationships together. Acts of *disloyalty* and acts of *betrayal* are those things that need to be forgiven! There may be others, but I believe most major hurts will fit into these two categories.

What is a "disloyal" act? A person is disloyal if he treats you like a stranger, when in fact, you belong as a friend, relative, or partner. Each one of us is bound to others by the invisible fibers of loyalty. The bonding tells us who we really are. That's why acts of disloyalty are so devastating. Words like "abandon" or

22

"forsake" or "let down" come to mind. One of the greatest acts of disloyalty ever recorded was when the Apostle Peter denied Jesus Christ three times before the rooster gave him his wake-up call.

You may have a partner, who has promised to come through with a loan, renege at the last moment because he can make a better deal...or a friend who promises to recommend you for a promotion and then "forgets" to do it when he discovers that the boss is interested in somebody else...or your father fails to show up at your graduation, special award ceremony, your big game, or your recital.

Turn the screws a bit tighter and disloyalty becomes betrayal. As disloyalty makes strangers of people who belong to each other, betrayal turns them into bitter enemies. We betray when we cut others to pieces. Peter was *disloyal* when he denied his Lord...but Judas *betrayed* Jesus when he turned Him over to His enemies. You betray me when you take a secret I entrusted you with and reveal it to someone else who, in turn, uses it against me. You betray when you, my best friend, whisper my secret shame to a gossiper. You betray when you are a brother/sister/spouse/cousin/friend who puts me down in front of significant people before whom I have no defense.

These all have the same feature: someone who is committed to be on your side turns against you like a sworn enemy. These are the kinds of things that need forgiveness. Let's not talk about forgiveness if there is no real pain.

POWER POINT: It's one thing to bless those who *irritate* you. It's an entirely different matter to bless those who *persecute* you! For those who irritate, just bless them in your heart and go on. For those who truly offend or even persecute you, proclaim your forgiveness verbally, to their face, and watch walls of resentment crumble before you!

Chapter 7

PRIMITIVE FORGIVING

The civilized cultures of this world are attempting in all kinds of ways to improve interpersonal relationships through all manner of methods. We are into justice for all, equality for all, and punishment for all those who do wrong. Maybe, just maybe, we should pause and take a look at the Babemba tribe of southern Africa, where there is a very primitive elementary criminal code which governs antisocial behavior. They have no fixed laws which are set in place to enforce justice. Apparently this lack comes from their close-knit community living which does not require such laws or justice system.

The source for this information is Brian Sharpe, who is the Director of the William Roper Hull Progressive Education Center headquartered in Calgary, Canada. He was reared among these tribes for the first nine years of his life. He shares with us the following information about how these tribes handle antisocial, delinquent, or criminal behaviors that are very infrequent. You shall soon discover why.

When a person in this tribe acts unjustly, he or she is placed in the center of the village, alone and unfettered. Work ceases as every person—adults and children—gather in a circle about the accused. Then, one by one, regardless of age, each takes their turn to relate, loudly enough so everyone can hear, about all the good things the accused person has done in their lifetime. All of the positive attributes, good deeds, strengths, and kindnesses are recited carefully and in great detail. However, no one is permitted to exaggerate, fabricate stories, or be facetious about the accomplishments or the positive aspects of the accused's character or their deeds.

This particular tribal ceremony will often last several days and is not concluded until everyone has been drained of every positive comment that can be mustered about the person in the middle of the circle. At the conclusion, this tribal circle is broken and a joyful celebration takes place. The person symbolically and literally is welcomed back into the tribe! Understand the full impact of this: NOT A WORD of criticism about him/her or the misdeed is allowed to be spoken!

Can you imagine what must be going through the mind of the person who is being subjected to such treatment? Think of the impact of being flooded with this wonderful warmth of tribal members—family and friends. This overwhelming bombardment can do nothing but strengthen a positive self-image and harden their resolve not only to avoid any misdeeds in the future but make them determined to live up to the expectations of his tribe in the future. Powerful!

Brian Sharpe also said that the need for such a ceremony is really quite rare. And we can easily see why. What a deterrent. Now…doesn't this account make you wonder a bit as to whether or not this so-called "primitive" society could teach us a whole lot of lessons on our subject at hand? We have our highly organized criminal and justice system firmly in place, but is it as powerful a deterrent as the tribal ceremony? Today we have an eye-for-an-eye kind of justice based on our legal traditions. If you had broken a law and experienced such a ceremony within your circle of important people in your life, what would be the effect on you and your future?

Let's take this another step. I'm wondering how this type of positive bombardment would work in miniature, as part of your family rituals and traditions. Yes! Why not? Aside from the obvious guilty feelings which we would hope, in turn, would result in the asking of forgiveness, it would also produce a profound sense of family. The accused would be reinforced in many ways, all positive. I believe it would bring about a strong awareness of who he or she is, why they are appreciated, and what is expected of them in the future. They would be better able to have the resolve to be productive and become more aware of what they have to offer to the world as well as to the family.

POWER POINT: The next time you feel like reacting to an offense, try the Babemba approach: Tell the offender everything you can think of to build him up. See what happens!

Chapter 8

IT'S RARE, DIFFICULT, AND COSTLY

"Will you forgive me?"

"Why of course! I've already forgiven you. Forget it; it didn't really matter. It didn't bother me."

What did I mean by that? The man had come to make a serious apology and what did I say? I let him know that I couldn't have cared less about what had happened; no big deal, it was nothing.

I felt quite good about it...until my conscience put on a demonstration by shouting: *Unfair! Hypocrite! Liar!*

What do you mean? Didn't I forgive the guy?

My conscience again said, *You just said you did...but you only winked at the offense and at him. You don't really know anything about forgiveness...at least not yet.*

That hurt because it was the truth. God sometimes has to teach us some hard lessons.

Forgiveness is rare. There is no real forgiveness in the cheap little game of looking the other way when

28

wrong has been committed. Forgiveness never just overlooks sin; it doesn't make light of wrong; it doesn't pretend that evil isn't evil; nor is it just politeness. It's not simply forgetting. The only way you can really forget a wrong done to you is when you have already forgiven the person who did it! To insist that forgetting comes first is to make passing the final exam the entrance requirement for the course. We've all been told by our mothers to simply "forgive and forget." But after you've tried to forget (without completely forgiving), you kick yourself over and over because you sometimes can't let go of the memory. The more you *try* to forget, the better your memory becomes. Forgetting is the *result* of complete forgiveness; it is never the *means*. It is the final step, not the first.

Never say: "Forget it...it's nothing," just to alleviate your conscience. To avoid or overlook evil is to be dishonest with yourself and the one who has wronged you. Sad to say, most people seem to prefer dishonesty in such matters, so no wonder forgiveness is really rare. It's rare because...

Forgiveness is DIFFICULT. True forgiveness is one of the hardest things to do. Our emotions tug at us, "Sure, he or she has wronged me...but let them pay!" When a betrayed trust or fractured relationship wallops us, we want to hold the grudge, then rush to the rescue to defend ourselves to the last word, to pin the blame where it's supposed to be!

Forgiveness short-circuits the part of our "self" which demands its "rights" by taking revenge or by playing the role of the pathetic victim, nursing the hurt for a long time. When you offer forgiveness, you can avoid this self-glorifying path that leads you nowhere. No wonder it's tough—you have to deny yourself to do it.

Forgiveness is difficult because…it is COSTLY. The person who is the forgiver pays a tremendous price! It's the price of evil that is forgiven. When the state pardons a criminal, society pays the burden. When a priceless, irreplaceable heirloom that has been a family treasure is broken, you may forgive the breaker, but you must pay the price by suffering the monetary loss of the item.

Suppose somebody ruins your reputation. To forgive that person means that you will still bear the long-term loss, and they will go scot-free. It's cutting the guilty person free from their deserved consequences.

It is outrageously costly because…all true forgiveness is SUBSTITUTIONAL. James Buswell writes: "All forgiveness, human and divine is, in the very nature of the case, vicarious, substitutional, and this is one of the most valuable views my mind has ever entertained. No one ever really forgives another, except he bears the penalty of the other's sin against himself."

This concept is freely expressed in the life of Jesus Christ. Jesus was the substitute for all of us…He bore the wrath of sin, His own indignation at sin, and paid the price we should have paid for our transgressions. God couldn't merely wink at our sins…they had to be atoned for. The cross is the eternal symbol of the price, the substitutional price, paid by Christ so that we could go free!

The following prayer was written in May, 1980, in Cyprus by Hassan B. Dehqani-Tafti, who was the President-Bishop of the Episcopal Church in Jerusalem and the Middle East and also Bishop in Iran.

A FATHER'S PRAYER
UPON THE MURDER OF HIS SON

O God,
We remember not only Bahram,
    but also his murderers.
Not because they killed him in the
    prime of his youth
And made our hearts bleed and our tears flow;
Not because with this savage act
    they have brought further
Disgrace on the name of our country
    among the civilized
Nations of the world;
But because through their crime we now follow
    Thy footsteps
More closely in the way of sacrifice.

The terrible fire of this calamity burns up all
Selfishness and possessiveness in us;
Its flame reveals the depth of depravity
    and meanness and suspicion,
The dimension of hatred and the measure
    of sinfulness in human nature;

31

It makes obvious as never before our need
    to trust in God's love
As shown in the Cross of Jesus and His Resurrection;
Love which makes us free from hate toward
    our persecutors;
Love which brings patience, forbearance,
    courage, loyalty,
Humility, generosity, greatness of heart.

Love which more than ever deepens our trust
    in God's final victory
And His eternal designs for the Church
    and for the world;
Love which teaches us how to prepare ourselves
    to face our own day of death.

O God,
Bahram's blood has multiplied the fruit of the Spirit
    in the soil of our souls;
So when the murderers stand before Thee
    on the day of Judgment
Remember the fruit of the Spirit by which
    they have enriched our lives,
And, forgive!

(*The Pastor's Story File*, April, 1986. Used by permission.)

⚡ POWER POINT: When someone asks for forgiveness, stop before quickly answering and consider how you would want them to respond if the roles
were reversed. Consider how much it cost them to do it.

Chapter 9

I'LL DO IT MY WAY

A man was quite surprised when his friend who was a minister gave up his pulpit to go back to school so he could practice medicine. The friend asked the former pastor why he had done it. "I took up the practice of medicine because I discovered that people will pay more money to care for their bodies than for their souls," was his answer.

Some years later the man gave up medicine and became an attorney. Perplexed, the friend asked for a reason and received this reply: "I took up the practice of law because I have discovered that people will pay more money to get their own way than for either body or soul."

Unfortunately, how right he is!

Countless numbers of people are ruining body, mind, and soul, and have no peace and joy because they are bent on making sure they have their own selfish ways! It's been said that a man is a fool who *can't* be angry, but that a man is wise who *won't* be angry.

It's at this juncture that we should pause and consider one of the most fantastic ways to ensure success in life or any kind of an endeavor you attempt. When we put God's way before our selfish ways, we do much to avoid unhappiness, insomnia, disease, and maybe even a lawsuit. This is so important that a reminder of it should be mounted on your bathroom mirror so you can see it first thing in the morning, on the dash of your car to remind yourself as you drive to work, and on your desk or work station so you can see it throughout the day.

In fact, you could build a very successful life and business based upon the following simple principle: "You have heard that it was said, 'Eye for eye, and tooth for tooth.' But I tell you, Do not resist an evil person. If someone strikes you on the right cheek, turn to him the other also. If someone forces you to go one mile, go with him two miles" (Matthew 5:38-39,41).

Foolish? Hardly, if because you walk an extra mile with someone, you find a new peace and joy in your life. All who have put this life principle into practice will testify to the refreshing medical, mental, physical, and spiritual benefits they have experienced. In giving this command, Jesus Christ must have also been thinking of our total well-being. But that is not all. He also said: "And if someone wants to sue you and take your tunic, let him have your cloak as well." (Matthew 5:40). Living like this may cost you more in your material goods...but what therapy for the soul. Let it go! Let them have it! This is an action of forgiveness in action.

34

Such a course of living can be hard on our pride. Too many of us would still rather "fight than switch," which in the long run can be disastrous to our well-being. Second-mile living is the only way to live if you value your health and happiness as well as your peace of mind.

Living like this is a choice! You must decide: either cater to your pride or preserve your mental, physical, and spiritual well-being!

This type of lifestyle may make you feel so good about yourself that you no longer need to stop at your local doctor's office to take that "shot" or prescription for your frazzled nerves. Going the second mile in all your relationships may allow you to feel better than ever in your life...in fact you may discover that the "pain" in your neck or back has also disappeared!

> He drew a circle that shut me out...
> Heretic, rebel, a thing to flout.
> But Love and I had the wit to win:
> We drew a circle that took him in.
> (Edwin Markham, "Outwitted")

Tough medicine? Sure...but only when all of us are living by this principle will there be true peace in this world!

(Matthew 5:38-41)

 POWER POINT: Consider how you can go the second mile with someone who has hurt you.

Chapter 10

WHAT IF IT REALLY HURTS?

How is it possible to forgive when the cost is absolutely staggering, when the pain is almost unbearable, and your hatred or anger is swelling and getting worse every day? Okay...how do you begin?

The mother, through tears, relates: "I'll never forget the look of white hot anger mingled with terror that filled Mindi's eyes that night. When she came through the door, all disheveled, I instinctively knew what had happened...it was like a nightmare coming to fruition."

It started when Mindi, an only child, began dating someone she had just met. Friends who had never before intruded in her life stopped by to drop a word of caution to her. No details, but a lot of vague warnings.

"We attempted to dissuade Mindi...but the opposition to their relationship only threw the two closer together. That night their intimacies had accelerated, Mindi attempted to stop it, he became violent, forced her, and then dropped her off some blocks from home, and fled town. He left her guilt-ridden, angry, depressed, violated, and pregnant! He was discovered to be with his father in another city and was brought back. He acted repentant and asked to see her alone to work things out. Instead he became violent and beat her severely enough to require days of hospitalization with concussions and shock. She wanted to die in her depression."

The boy? A few weeks in detention and a couple of interviews with a psychiatrist, and he was set free only to get another girl pregnant. He immediately made plans to marry this new girl.

Mindi's mother and father continued to lie awake at night, burning with anger and bitterness. The baby was adopted by a family, and Mindi is recovering. She's entered another college in another state, but the scars go deep. The old buoyancy is gone forever…there's no more trust left in her.

The mother says: "I can't possibly express the intense feelings I have toward this thing that has ruined all of our lives. Isn't there some way this hurt can be healed? Is there forgiveness for things this big and terrifying?"

Can this act of forgiveness be accomplished alone? No! It takes at least two to work through a serious matter of forgiveness—God and you! Where else can you get the strength to pull something like this off? The secret is God working in and through you to lead you to the point of forgiving. "Work out the salvation that God has given you with a proper sense of awe and responsibility. For it is God who is at work within you, giving you the will and power to achieve His purpose" (Philippians 2:12-13, Phillips Translation).

Okay…where do you begin when it's this tough?

Begin with an understanding of the other person. What? Impossible! Consider…don't brush this off by thinking this scum bag doesn't need your understanding before you judge and hang him in the court of your mind. Try…just try for a tiny bit. There is usually a reason behind every action, not that this will excuse the terrible act.

Understanding is the foundation which underlies forgiveness. The real purpose of understanding is only to help us to see the difference between what the sinner DID and what/who the sinner IS! Yes…that person may have done horrible things that are grossly wrong…but there is more to that person than the misdeeds. Any understanding of him is an impossibility without God's help in your life.

Along this line, there is a second step—learning how to value others. Take another look at this despicable, horrible, scum bag of wretched humanity. No matter how horrible or how bad his actions, this person is a human being…a human being for whom Jesus Christ also died. I remind you that the highest unit of value in the universe is the human soul! No one—I repeat—no one for whom Christ died is to be the object of hate. Every person is meant to be a child of God. Before you totally write this person off and refuse to forgive, stop and think. No person is too low to be an object of God's love! No one is to be excluded from the forgiveness which only God can offer! No one is to be considered worthless for whom Christ has died! No one is beyond the love of God! NO ONE!

Ralf Luther put it like this: "To love one's enemy does not mean to love the mire in which the pearl lies, but to love the pearl that lies in the mud."

(Philippians 2:12-13)

⚡ POWER POINT: Look at your list of those who have offended you. Consider what you already know about them that will help you understand their actions. Then begin to pray for them!

Chapter 11

WHAT EXACTLY DO WE DO?

There is one anxiety which dominates most of our living. What is it? Most of us are anxious in the face of our unchangeable past. How we long to be able to recreate segments of our private histories, but we are stuck with them. "But God..."—isn't that a wonderful phrase? Yes, God has the answer to this anxiety. God is a forgiving God who recreates our past by forgiving us! And by His grace, we too, can participate in His power to change the past. We, too, *can* and *must* forgive. By sharing in this divine power, we become most powerfully human and most wonderfully free. It works like a miracle cure.

Hannah Arendt, the Jewish philosopher, wrote a book, *The Human Condition* and in it addresses the power of the human spirit. She concludes that only when we act after the fashion of the biblical Lord can we overcome our darkest forbodings. "There is," she writes, "only one remedy for the inevitability of history: FORGIVENESS!"

In the natural course of life we are stuck with our past and its effects on us. We can learn from our personal history, but we can't escape it. We attempt to forget our history, but we can't change it. We may be doomed to repeat it, but we can't change it. Our past is a part of our being. There is only one thing that can release us from the grip of our personal history. Jesus urges us to forgive for even far greater reasons than our histories: "When you stand praying, if you hold anything against anyone, forgive him, so that your Father in heaven may forgive you your sins" (Mark 11:25).

So...exactly what do we do when we forgive? There are at least three stages in every act of forgiveness: suffering, spiritual surgery, and starting all over again.

The first stage, *suffering*, creates the conditions that require forgiveness. Here is where the pain happens; the hurt is inflicted; the dastardly deed has been performed. No one really has the right to forgive unless they have been hurt; otherwise, we turn this miracle into nothing more than a cheap ritual.

At the second stage, *spiritual surgery*, we do the essential business of forgiving, which is a cutting away of the memory in our own mind.

Let's take a more intense look at the spiritual surgery involved. This stage takes in the hurt person's inner response to the guilty party. When you forgive, you slice away the wrong from the person who did the deed! You disengage that person from the harmful act. You are performing surgery on your memory. At one moment you identify that person as the dirty rascal

41

who did you wrong…in this next critical moment you change that identity. This person is remade in your memory! You no longer think of this person as someone whom you hate, but rather someone who needs you and your forgiveness.

You recreate your past by recreating this person in your own memory! God does it just like this, too. He releases you from your sin like your mother washed the dirt off your body when you were a child.

You also need to know…sometimes this is only as far as we can go. Sometimes we need to forgive people who are dead and gone. Sometimes we must forgive people who don't want our forgiveness. Sometimes our forgiving has to end with what happens in the spiritual surgery of our own memories. In order to pull this off, God must give us the strength, and He has promised He would. It's quite simple—we make the choice to do it, and God provides the grace and strength to pull it off!

The miracle is completed when two people who have become alienated *start all over again*. You can do it! It will happen!

The process is quite simple and easily understood, but we are so human, so prone to doing it our way, which is a totally fruitless exercise. But the possibilities that it holds are endless…

(Mark 11:25)

POWER POINT: Are there those you need to forgive who have passed on or are beyond the possibility of communication? Write them a letter of forgiveness and then burn it before the Lord!

42

Chapter 12

A QUIET ACT OF FORGIVENESS

Many years ago, a simple, quiet act of forgiveness began a chain of events that survives to this day.

Our story begins deep within one of those infamous Siberian prison camps. A Jew by the name of Dr. Boris Kornfeld was imprisoned there along with hundreds of other inmates. Because he was a medical doctor he was forced into performing surgeries and other medical services for the staff and prisoners. When not in surgery, he was forced to help the prison staff as they demanded. As he was working with a prisoner, he discovered him to be a Christian, an anonymous forgotten man, whose quiet faith in the face of being imprisoned made an impression on the doctor. The one thing that particularly touched Dr. Kornfeld was his frequent reciting of the "Lord's Prayer."

One day, while repairing a guard's artery, which had been cut in a knifing, the doctor seriously considered suturing it in such a way that he would bleed to death a short while after the operation. Appalled by the hatred and violence he saw in his own heart, he found himself repeating the words of the nameless prisoner: "Forgive us our sins as we forgive those who sin against us."

Shortly after that secret prayer, Dr. Kornfeld began to refuse to go along with some of what were the standard practices of the prison camp. Among other things the doctor did because of his new-found faith was to turn in an orderly who had been stealing food from dying patients. Following that, he knew his life was in danger, so he began to spend as much time as possible in the relative safety of the prison hospital.

One afternoon he was examining a patient whom he had just operated on for cancer of the intestines. This was a man whose eyes and face reflected a depth of spiritual misery, physical misery, and emptiness that touched and moved Kornfeld. So the doctor began talking to the patient, telling him about the Christian patient. After sensing the man's positive response, he continued and told the prisoner the entire story, including his incredible confession of secret faith in Jesus Christ.

That night, under cover of darkness, when nobody else was around, someone, most likely the orderly, crept in and smashed Dr. Kornfeld's head with a club while he was asleep. He died a few short hours later, never regaining consciousness.

But the testimony of Kornfeld did not die! As a result of his confession, the cancer patient who had listened became a Christian. And he managed to survive that prison camp and later went on to write a book about the experience in which he told the world what he had learned there.

Who is this patient who survived cancer, became a Christian, survived the Siberian prison labor camp, and wrote the book? We know him today as the great writer, Aleksandr Solzhjenitsyn!

(Adapted, Charles Colson, *Loving God*, Zondervan, Grand Rapids, MI, 1990.)

⚡ POWER POINT: Have the people of your ethnic group been maligned, ostracized, or taken advantage of by bigots or other segments of our society? If so, you may need to write a letter of forgiveness to them (see previous Power Point).

Chapter 13

HOW DO WE FORGIVE?

None of us really knows how to forgive without help from God. In attempting to do it, most of us are like fumbling amateurs, but we must endeavor to do it anyway. However, I've noticed some things about people who do the forgiving.

People sometimes forgive slowly. There are some people who are "instant" forgivers, but they usually have learned how to do it. (We will discuss this further in the next chapter.) When we first begin to make forgiveness an intricate part of our lifestyle, we should not count on the power to forgive painful hurts very quickly.

C.S. Lewis tells about the monster of a teacher he had when he was a schoolboy. He hated this academic sadist most of his life. But a few months before he died, he wrote to an American friend: "Dear Mary...do you know, only a few weeks ago, I realized suddenly that I had at last forgiven the cruel schoolmaster who so darkened my childhood. I had been trying to do it for years."

God takes His time with lots of things…perhaps you need some time for this miracle of forgiveness to happen in your life. Please, don't throw in the sponge if you find that you can't do it quickly or as soon as you think it should be offered. If it takes some time, so be it…but keep on with the process.

People forgive with the help of others. Really, can anyone forgive alone? I don't think they can. I need people to be with me who have hurt as I have hurt…who have hated as I have hated…who have struggled as I have struggled…before I can manage to forgive. It's great if you can do it all by yourself…but if you are still hooked into the videotape of your past pain, seek a fellowship of slow forgivers. They may help. And always, as we forgive and when we forgive, the greatest help will be God's help.

People forgive as they are forgiven. When it comes right down to it, anyone who forgives can hardly tell the difference between *feeling* forgiven and *doing* the forgiving. We are such a mixture of sinners and sinned against that we cannot forgive people who offend us without feeling that we have been set free ourselves.

Corrie Ten Boom is an example of this truth. It was my privilege to hear her speak in Milwaukee before she passed on. She shared with us the following story.

While imprisoned in a concentration camp in World War II, she was humiliated and degraded, especially in the delousing shower where the women were ogled by the leering, lecherous guards. She managed to make it through that hell and eventually felt she had, by God's grace, forgiven them all, even those fiends who guarded the shower stalls.

Afterwards, she traveled the world, preaching forgiveness not just for individuals but for all of Europe. One Sunday in Munich, following her message as she was greeting the people, she saw a man come toward her, hand outstretched: "Ja, Fraulein, it is wonderful that Jesus forgives us all our sins, just as you say." Then she remembered his face—it was the leering, lecherous, mocking face of one of the SS guards in the shower stall!

Corrie says that her hand froze at her side; she could not reach out to him, although she thought she had forgiven it all. But she found that she had not forgiven this guard when she saw him standing in front of her. Ashamed, horrified at herself, she prayed: "Lord, forgive me; I cannot forgive!"

As she prayed, she felt forgiven and accepted in spite of her shabby performance as a "world-class famous forgiver." Her hand was suddenly unfrozen, the ice of hate melted, and her hand went out. She said that she forgave as she was forgiven and was not able to sort out the difference!

Forgiveness sets us free, free at last! Thank God Almighty, we *are* free at last! Freed by the only remedy for the inevitability of our painful past history!

To FORGIVE is like putting down your 50 pound pack after a 10 mile hike up the side of a mountain!

To FORGIVE is like falling into a chair after running a 26-mile marathon!

To FORGIVE is setting the prisoner free and discovering in reality that the prisoner was you!

To FORGIVE is reaching back into your hurting past and recreating it in your memory so that you can begin again by consciously letting go of the pain!

To FORGIVE is dancing to the beat of God's forgiving heart!

To FORGIVE is riding the crest of love's strongest wave!

To FORGIVE is approaching the attributes of God Himself!

To FORGIVE is preparing to enter future creative possibilities!

To FORGIVE is experiencing the miracle of God's grace!

POWER POINT: If you're having trouble forgiving someone, put them on your "People I Need to Forgive" list. This establishes your intent, even if your feelings aren't up to it. The next step is to reach out to them. You won't be able to stay angry with them for very long if you engage in meaningful contact.

Chapter 14

IT'S A FREE GIFT OR IT'S NOTHING

"Sure…I'll forgive him, but not until I'm good and ready!" she spat out as the three of us sat about the table…husband, wife, and pastor. The teakettle whistled on the stove, the man in question sat with eyes fastened on the floor, silent before her anger.

She continued, "If only you knew how much misery he's caused me, you might understand why I'm not going to submit or knuckle under when he says 'sorry' for the first time!" She paused, eyes flashing, face flushed with anger, chin quivering with emotion, then continued, "Sure, I'll forgive him, but not until he's paid and paid dearly for the dirt he's dragged us through!"

Earlier in the week she and her daughter had tracked down the "other" woman in her husband's life, rang the doorbell, and waited. The other woman stood framed in the doorway, her welcoming smile frozen on her face when she recognized her callers. They all stood in mutual hate. The daughter broke the spell. "I've wanted to see your face for years, and now that I've seen it," she spit in her face, "you make me sick!"

Years passed...this other woman moved out of town. Slowly, painfully, bitterly, the husband paid, repaid, and overpaid for what he had done. At long last, one night, when the wife was in deep pain, lonely, bitter, sick, friendless...she offered her forgiveness. Too late!

He told her, "You can just keep your phony forgiveness. I don't need it now because I have already paid through the nose for what I did. Who needs forgiveness when he's already paid the price?"

Who indeed? Forgiveness is a free gift or it amounts to nothing at all! It is not to be a receipt for payment in full. It's an undeserved pardon, an unwarranted release, with no strings attached...or it's not genuine forgiveness.

Although you may naturally be a slow forgiver as we discussed in the last chapter, it's so much better if you can *learn to forgive immediately*. However, when you make the choice to postpone forgiveness until the last angry installment has been extracted, complete with interest, it's not forgiveness—it's pure revenge! If you purposely hold back your forgiveness until the offender "deserves it," you might as well not go through the motions—that's getting even, exacting a "pound of flesh" as Shakespeare's merchant of Venice tried to do.

Learn to forgive immediately...or at least begin

the process of forgiveness as quickly as possible. Forgive when the hurt is first felt. The people who follow the example of Jesus Christ will hurry to forgive, quickly, unhesitatingly, completely, and immediately! Time is of great value in forgiveness…it's so easy to let the opportunity slip away without responding to the hurt.

It is much less costly to pardon than it is to nurture resentment. The person who learns to forgive before the sting has swollen, before the molehill becomes a mountain, or before bitterness becomes an infection, is a blessed person.

Learn to forgive before bitterness sets in. Bitterness is a strange thing…it breaks over us when we least need it, when we're down and in desperate need of all of our freedoms, abilities, and energies to get back up after the blow. What strange things bitterness does to us—our feelings can become hardened around us like a plaster cast that restricts movement. Bitterness causes paralysis of the soul!

A young man who is falsely accused, condemned, and penalized by a boss turns sullen, angry, and bitter. His faith in all justice and authority dies. He will not forgive nor attempt to forget. His career may be forever on hold.

A girl becomes pregnant and is abandoned by the man whom she trusted, whom she planned on marrying. She withdraws from life and turns bitter. Her faith in humanity ends. Unable to trust another man, she throws away any chances she may have for a normal family life for her and her child. She, too, will not forgive.

A businessman catches a trusted employee embezzling his carefully nurtured business. He turns sour on all humanity and becomes an inward, selfish, impossible boss to the rest of his employees. If his business survives, it will do only that—survive. Chances are good that it probably will not prosper. He will not forgive, either.

WHY DO WE ACCEPT BITTERNESS WHEN WE COULD FORGIVE?

⚡ POWER POINT: Do you have a root of bitterness toward someone that is poisoning your life and those closest to you? If you can't handle it yourself, consider obtaining professional help: counseling, prayer, or other ministry!

Chapter 15

HOW OFTEN?

Jesus spoke quite often about forgiveness. One time Peter boldly asked, "Lord, how many times shall I forgive my brother when he sins against me?" Peter, it seems, without a pause answered his own question. How interesting. There might have been more than a bit of pride as he supplied his own answer, "Up to seven times?" Where did he get this number seven from? Well…Jewish law said that three times was enough when offering forgiveness. So seven times must have seemed magnanimous to Peter.

But Jesus shook His head and answered, "I tell you, not seven times, but seventy times seven!" Seventy multiplied by seven—490 times—this must have stunned the disciple.

And as Peter was mulling this over, Jesus told an interesting story about a man who owed the king more than 10 thousand talents…an amount which today would total in the millions of dollars. Since this sum was way beyond the ability of the borrower to repay, the king ordered the man, his wife, and all his children, even babies, to be sold into slavery so that some of the debt could be paid.

The man fell to his knees before the king, took the king's hand in his as tears spilled out, and begged, "Be patient with me, and I will pay back everything." Anyone could easily see that this offer of his was an impossibility. But the king was moved with compassion, took pity on the servant, and canceled the entire debt! Awesome!

End of story? Not hardly. As the man was on his way home, no doubt to break the good news to his wife and family, he found a man who owed him 100 denarii, not much more than about $20 in today's currency. Grabbing him by the neck, he began to choke the man, demanding payment! The debtor begged for mercy and a bit more time, but instead, the man had him thrown into prison until the debt was paid in full.

What an ungrateful wretch...but you can't keep news like this covered for long. Other people, who had seen what had happened, told the king the whole story. The king immediately sent for the man who had been forgiven. "You wicked servant, I canceled all that debt of yours because you begged me to. Shouldn't you have had mercy on your fellow servant just as I had on you?" The forgiven man was sent to the torture chambers until he paid every bit of the debt!

Take special note of the following conclusion: "Jesus continued, 'This is how my heavenly Father will treat each of you unless you forgive your brother from your heart!'" (Matthew 18:23-35)

Every one of us is in the position of the man who owed the huge, unpayable debt. Every day we need to experience God's forgiveness. We are so human, so frail. Now...let's be honest with ourselves. Aren't we guilty of committing sins...sins committed with our bodies as well as our minds and mouths? We have sinned in our failure to do right and sinned when we have chosen second best. But no matter what we have done, God is ready to forgive when we ask Him!

The question of forgiveness is not about God nor His willingness to forgive. The real crux of this matter is whether or not we will ask Him for forgiveness. Lots of people are still suffering because they have chosen to believe that God cannot forgive them. Have you been one of those who has committed a sin so horrible that you think it unforgivable? IF... IF...you have sincerely asked God's forgiveness, YOU ARE FORGIVEN!!! God's forgiveness is 100%! The Bible tells us even though our sins have been like scarlet...they shall become white as snow! (Isaiah 1:18) He promised that our confessed sins will be removed as far from Him as the east is from the west!

Perhaps this is the moment for us to pause for prayer. "Dear God...thank you for creating me. Thank you for loving me the way I am. Thank you for changing my life for the better. And most of all, I thank you for forgiving my sins as I have asked your forgiveness. Amen."

It is only when we have experienced the awe-inspiring, life-changing forgiveness of God that we, in turn, can bestow our forgiveness upon others.

(Matthew 18:21-35)

⚡ POWER POINT #1: Are you in need of God's forgiveness? Did you pray the prayer on the previous page? No matter how many times you've sinned, He is ready to extend forgiveness and a fresh start!

⚡ POWER POINT #2: If you'd like to have a reminder to forgive seventy times seven times, a t-shirt with "70 Times Seven" is available from the publisher of this book. Call 888-670-7463 for more information.

Chapter 16

I WANT TO, BUT…

Have you ever said, "I want to forgive him or her. I know I should, but how can I?"

Or…"I'll never be able to forgive myself!"

Or…"How can I ever forgive You, God, for letting such a thing happen to me?"

Nobody but nobody can do your forgiving for you! Yet, too often we have been caught in the I can't/won't forgive trap.

There is not a person among us who doesn't need to be forgiven because the Bible says, "for all have sinned and fall short…" (Romans 3:23). But at the same time we have a mandate to "Be kind and compassionate to one another, forgiving each other…" (Ephesians 4:32).

But that's not all. From childhood most of us have learned to repeat the Lord's Prayer. We have repeated many times, "Forgive us our debts, as we also have forgiven our debtors" (Matthew 6:12). But…what about putting those principles and that prayer into practice? It's a simple concept…but tough living it out in real life.

I know it's a hard thing to do…but making that first move can go an awful long way toward restoring inner peace. It might take more than one encounter to finally achieve forgiveness and peace of mind.

Forgiveness can be called the very *highest form of giving*. And to all of us to whom much has been given, from us much shall be required.

There's another thing to consider: Upon reading the Bible, which is the guide to repairing all relationships, the concept of forgiveness seems to be turned around. YOU are instructed to make the first move toward the one who has something against you even if, in reality, you have done nothing wrong to them. Reconciliation is the important thing here. "If you are offering your gift at the altar and there remember that your brother has something against you, leave your gift there in front of the altar. First go and be reconciled to your brother; then come and offer your gift" (Matthew 5:23-24).

Why isn't it the responsibility of the person who has been avoiding you or accusing you of evil to make things right? That kind of a procedure seems to make more sense, doesn't it? But that is not what Jesus said to do. YOU go! YOU make the first move! YOU are to initiate the reconciliation. "But it's not fair…" you can protest. It makes no difference. YOU are to be the one; the first move is yours!

How you approach them will determine to a great degree whether or not your effort will result in reconciliation or more hostility. It's more than simply going.

When you go to them, you must go with the right kind of attitude. For example…

A young man who was no longer willing to live with the friction between him and his mother-in-law decided to take the first step to remedy the situation. It ended in more disaster! Why? The so-called "peacemaker," in a brusque, sharp, hard tone of voice, began with: "Isn't it about time you get over whatever you have against me?"

The mother-in-law's response was equally belligerent. "Why should I?" And the battle lines were more firmly drawn! Anybody could have predicted such an outcome with such an attitude. He was right to make the first move, but…!

Contrast the above with the unhappy younger woman who also made up her mind to do something to improve the situation between herself and her mother-in-law. She first prayed that she might have a calm, peaceful spirit, and above all set a guard over her tongue. Then she stopped at the florist to select a beautiful potted plant, her mother-in-law's favorite. The older woman's what-do-you-think-you-have-come-for look did nothing to encourage the daughter-in-law.

But the young woman began, "Mom, I'm not sure what it is, but I must have done something to hurt you, and I want to ask you to forgive me. I love you and I want us to get back to being a family again. Can't we…" She never finished; her words were lost as the older woman reached out her arms and together they hugged and shed tears.

About now I'm hearing someone say, "But what if my offer is refused?" That makes no difference! The Bible gives us no guarantee that the person we make the first move toward will receive us. But of this you can be sure—as you make the first move, as you express it, you will experience peace and a flood of God-given joy! This biblical doctrine of forgiveness is the most liberating, joy-restoring truth in the whole Bible!

You can "What if?" your way through life, rationalizing and failing to obey God and His Word, or you can risk taking that very first step of forgiveness and begin reaping the rewards!

But, what if…you don't!?!

(Matthew 5:23-24)

⚡ POWER POINT: When you take the "first step" with someone whom you believe also must bear responsibility in the offense, do it unilaterally. That is, do not expect or ask them to reciprocate (ask for your forgiveness as well). Remember it's not a negotiation—it's a simple act of admitting your error, even if you're only 1% at fault!

Chapter 17

DO YOU NEED IT?

Are you fighting an inner battle with a memory from the past? Is the skeleton in one of yesterday's closets beginning to rattle? Guilt and anxiety could be drilling holes in your hull, and you may be sinking in your own fears. Maybe an inner voice is shouting, "You'll never be able to soar again! It's over with! What will happen when they find out about it?"

Destructive thoughts? Yes! Merciless accusers? Yes! You may have done or experienced things that if they became public knowledge could destroy you, your family, or your reputation. It may be a hidden criminal record, moral charge, or domestic conflict that you have kept private. You may be wrestling with a past when you were deeply wounded; maybe you have had a mental breakdown or been involved with drug abuse. You might have attempted suicide. You might live with memories that have become covered with the sands of time. You may be covering an illicit relationship, a financial failure, a terrible habit, a theft, or have been on the run. You might be sensing that any one or more of these things would mar or cripple you if their dirty details were ever spilled out in front of gossipers.

Hold on, my friend. Before you give up, let's take a look at some of the people who were used by God in spite of their pasts.

Abraham...the founder and father of Israel, the man who was called the "friend of God," lied and deceived an ungodly king in Egypt in order to save his hide and that of his beautiful wife Sarai. There's more...he fathered a son, Ishmael, through his wife's slave who grew up to become the archenemy of the Jewish people to this day. (Ishmael became father of the Arabs.)

Joseph...had a prison record. He was an unmitigated spoiled brat. Yet he rose to become Prime Minister in Egypt and was the man who saved the infant nation of Israel from extinction.

Moses...committed murder! In a fit of anger, he killed an Egyptian and then became a runaway who fled for his life. This man later led his people out of their Egyptian bondage.

Jephthah...was an illegitimate kid who led a gang of the toughest hombres, the "Hell's Angels" of his day. Later God chose him to lead his nation in a glorious military victory which meant deliverance for his people.

Rahab...was a harlot, a common prostitute in the streets of Jericho. She delivered her family from a sure death and later was used in such a mighty way that she is listed in God's hall of fame in Hebrews 11.

Samson...a he-man with a she-habit. He was a "Nazarite" who turned his back on his vows to spend time with the prostitutes of his day. He lost his eyes...yet was used to bring about one of the greatest victories of deliverance the nation of Israel experienced over the Philistines.

Are you still unconvinced? The list isn't finished. It's really quite long. Let's look at a few more...

Eli and Samuel...were poor, inconsistent, and failures as fathers and family men. Yet they proved to be strong men under the direction of God's leading.

Jonah and John Mark...were missionaries who ran away from their responsibilities and places of ministry because of hardships. Yet, they came back to be mightily used of God later on.

Peter...poor Peter. Everyone in the world is aware of his public denials of his Lord. He openly cursed the Lord—only, later, to become one of God's choicest servants in leading the infant church. He also wrote two very important books of the Bible.

Paul...was the number one persecutor of the early Church. He threw people into prison, killed others, stoned some, and was so feared that, following his conversion, the disciples at first refused to have anything to do with him. You know the rest of the story...he became the greatest spokesman for the Gospel the world has ever known and the most prolific writer to the new Church.

Our list is not nearly exhausted yet. The record-books of heaven are filled with true-life stories of people who were renegades, rebels, and scoundrels. The change came with God's FORGIVENESS! They became redeemed, refitted, and rewarded!

My friend...are you in need of God's forgiveness? It's a matter of asking for it!

⚡ POWER POINT: Plan now to get away for a few hours or even a day to be alone with the Lord. Use this time to re-connect with Him. Open yourself up to God's searchlight. Let Him show you areas that He wants to change. Then ask for His forgiveness and cleansing. If your repentance is sincere, He will grant it!

Chapter 18

WHAT ABOUT CONFESSING?

Is it possible to find forgiveness without first making an honest confession? What do you do with what has been done? What if your sin is so personal and so painful that you don't want to share it with anyone else? How can guilt be dealt with before there is a confession? Interesting questions, don't you think? What if what we have done needs to be made right?

If a person repents—honestly and completely—and turns from the past and its sins, must there also be a confession to the one who was hurt? Honest confession can bring a tremendous sense of relief, but what then? Will the person to whom the confession is made be able to forgive, forget, and accept again? Or will the confession simply be another obstacle in the relationship? I don't know if I can supply all the answers to these questions, but I suggest the following as guidelines:

Confession should be as public as the sin. Only those directly involved should be told in your confessing. Sin need not be published for general public consumption and speculation. Don't satisfy the morbid curiosity of people not a part of the problem or situation.

Confession should only be shared when it can be a help. Often, a confession will hurt more or be a hindrance to future relationships. Sometimes the confession will provide another with an excuse to retaliate or create a further temptation to be explored. Will your confession cause another to stumble? It's at this point that I have some real concerns about "celebrity" type people who are invited to our church pulpits to parade their sordid past as their "personal testimony."

Confession should not be so intimate that it will scar others. A confession can be so revealing, so intimate, so painful, so emotional, that it will scar the person or persons who hear the confession. Such careless or thoughtless confession to a close friend or spouse may bring you a release but transfers the painful burden to another. Do you really want to be healed at the expense of another's suffering?

If you choose not to confess for the sake of being redemptive, be aware that you are choosing the more difficult way. To live with an unshared memory of your sin, to find forgiveness without sharing the meaning of that forgiveness, is not the easier way. It can be all the more demanding of you and your spiritual maturity. That is true...but also remember that confession is a human necessity. Always confess to God, but think again before confessing it to others.

We discover and experience release from our guilt in direct proportion to our willingness to face our sin, confess our sinfulness, and accept God's forgiveness. In any honest confession, we turn ourselves inside out.

Confession has two sides. It can be an "admit-your-failures-and-get-them-off-your-chest" variety, or it can be a confession of dependence and allegiance to God who is the great guilt-remover. Let's take a closer look at these two sides.

There must be a confession of sinfulness. Admit it! That's a necessary step. Guilt wants to stay hidden. It breeds best in isolation. It prefers the dark unswept corners of your personality. It eats away like termites and destroys most completely when hidden. But when brought to the light, its power crumbles.

David described the bone-rot of guilt: "When I kept silent, my bones wasted away...my strength was sapped" (Psalm 32:3-4). His confession was not the shallow, "Dear-God-I-goofed-again" sort. His confession went to the root of sin. (Read the entire 32nd Psalm.) Can you be that honest before God?

Then there must be the confession of surrender. This is the positive side. To find real release from guilt, you must also confess your faith and your surrender. "You must confess with your own mouth that Jesus Christ is your Lord and believe in your heart. For it is by believing in his heart that a man becomes right with God and with his mouth he confesses his faith" (Romans 10:9-10, paraphrased).

The greatest, clearest moment of truth open to any person happens when we see ourselves as we are seen in Jesus Christ. As confession is made, we come face to face with what truth demands.

A.W. Tozer describes this moment: "The man on the cross is facing in only one direction. He is not going back and he has no plans of his own."

In confession, we trade an old self-centered life for His new life and confess the need for Him to control our new life.

When we reaffirm our confession of Jesus as our Lord and Savior, we are reaffirming our place as a child of God and heir to His Kingdom. Only when we take our place with Him as a redeemed person whose slate is once again wiped clean, can we truly begin to deal with the guilt that we may feel is still attached to us.

(Psalm 32; Romans 10:9-10)

⚡ POWER POINT: When you can't confess to someone because it would hurt them more than help them, consider confiding in your pastor, mentor, or close friend who can be trusted to maintain confidentiality.

Chapter 19

IT'S TIME TO FORGIVE YOURSELF

Guilt has a way of eating away at your insides, attacking your nerves, and causing sleepless nights. It makes you jumpy. What happens when the phone rings, there is a knock at your door, an official looking letter arrives? Do meals taste like sawdust? These could well be only the beginning if you continue to ignore your responsibility to yourself.

Guilt causes an escapee to hide from the police. A student unprepared to answer looks away from the teacher. A child sulks in their room behind a closed door. The person who feels guilty, unforgiven, will do all that is possible to avoid a confrontation with God. Adam and Eve disobeyed and attempted to hide.

The important thing is that something must be done to relieve us of our guilt! It may not be easy! Oh, let's be honest...it is not easy for me and neither for you. But it can be done!

Let's start with...

CONFESSION

As we have seen in the previous chapter, we have a built-in resistance to admitting personal failures, shouldering guilt, and accepting personal responsibility for our actions. However, this is the place to start, difficult or not. Articulate these four words: "I made a mistake!" Tell God: "I sinned!" Until you have cleared this hurdle and opened the door of your heart, you will still be locked into guilt. Denial, in any form, is not confession.

Seneca, the Roman philosopher who lived about the same time as Christ, put it very bluntly: "Why does no one confess his vices? Because he is still in them! It is the one who wakes that reports the dream."

RESTITUTION

Step two isn't much easier. God has forgiven you, and others may have forgiven you, but somehow you can't forgive yourself. What should you do? Make restitution in some way. Send an E-mail, make a phone call, write a letter, make a visit, replace or fix something if that's appropriate, and above all, pray! In your praying, ask God to help you make the correct restitution. Pray His blessings on the person you wronged even as you are seeking forgiveness for yourself.

RECOVERY

It may not happen quickly, but healing is a process. Here are some practical things you can do.

Think through them as you read. It's at this point that you might want to slow your pace…reflect upon each idea, think of how you can make an application to your situation.

1) Determine whether the guilt you are struggling with is authentic or counterfeit. Face it…a whole lot of misery is caused by standards that are completely off the scale. Have you exaggerated it all out of proportion? If so, your guilt can become neurotic. Counterfeit guilt is generated by the imagination. It's the proverbial molehill being made into a mountain in your mind. Are others telling you that you should feel guilty? Don't let anyone except God set the standard for your conscience.

2) Be contrite for the right thing. What do people most often regret? Yes, unfortunately they regret that they got caught! Being sorry you got caught is not nearly as helpful as being sorry you made the wrong choice in the first place.

3) Be submissive to Christ. Christ told us the "Comforter" would be our helper. The original Greek word for comforter is "paraclete," meaning "the one called to the side of." A comforter is a helper. It's time to cooperate with the Spirit of God working in your life.

4) Take another look at the offense from Christ's perspective. This time, as you return to the scene of the "crime," take Jesus Christ with you. Examine it once more in the bright light of His presence. He will not pound you over the head with a mallet and berate

you for making another mess. He always specializes in "Plan B." His specialty is turning something negative into something positive.

5) Change your lifestyle. The Jesus who forgave sin never once told the sinner to keep on doing it. To the woman caught in adultery He said, after He had forgiven her, "go and sin no more!" (John 8:10-11) Continue on your journey...but don't keep stumbling over the same stones.

However, you're not quite home free yet! You have more to do. Being a human being, you'll most likely stumble again. That statement is not meant to be pessimistic. It's a fact, and we must acknowledge it. Accepting God's forgiveness and forgiving yourself will not make you perfect, yet. Sorry about that. This journey is about falling down, getting up, falling down, getting up...all the way to heaven! YOU CAN FORGIVE YOURSELF and keep on trucking!

(John 8:10-11)

⚡ POWER POINT: Most of us don't plan to fail, but we do fail to plan! Over the next few days, think about how you can restructure your life so as to avoid the situations that so easily trip you up.

73

Chapter 20

INVEST IN YOUR OFFENDER

Here is a step that is almost always overlooked by those who are seeking to have a forgiving spirit. This is a real key to turning bitterness into forgiveness and forgiveness into genuine love. It's very rare. What is it? Voluntarily investing in the life of your offender!

Two brothers were farmers, specializing in growing rice, and they were also committed Christians who were sincerely attempting to be Christ-like in all their dealings with others. They were startled one morning to discover that the water they had pumped into one of their fields had been drained off by their neighbor into his field. His field was a little lower than theirs, and he had made a cut in their dike. The brothers forgave their neighbor in their hearts and expressed it verbally to each other. Then they repaired the broken dike and pumped up more water. (For you who might not be farmers, rice is grown in fields of standing water.)

For the next several nights, their neighbor continued to drain off their water into his field. Finally, the brothers went to their pastor and asked, "Why don't we have joy and love in our hearts for our neighbor when we have forgiven him?"

The pastor wisely replied, "You'll never have joy or love for your neighbor until you begin irrigating his field for him!" This idea sounded utterly preposterous to the farmer-brothers. But driving home in their pick-up, they decided to give it a try.

The next day they made a marvelous discovery! The longer they worked on their neighbor's field, irrigating it, the more joy they had in the Lord, and the more their love for their neighbor grew.

But the story doesn't end there. It goes on to a most interesting conclusion. After irrigating their neighbor's field for several days, he finally came to them, told them that he couldn't stand it any longer, and confessed his wrongdoing, asking for their forgiveness. As a result of this incident, they were able to help him to become a Christian.

Talk about radical!

Now, wait a minute...radical, yes! But can you imagine what kind of an impact this sort of radical forgiveness would have on others in this world?

What's this strange concept and how does it work? Jesus, in the historic "Sermon on the Mount," stated that, "Where your treasure is, there your heart will be also" (Matthew 6:21). Therefore, when the brothers invested in their neighbor, they found that a portion of their treasure, and also their hearts, were now invested with their miserable neighbor.

This is the same life principle in action when Jesus taught, "If someone forces you to go one mile, go with him two miles" (Matthew 5:41). In Christ's day, there was a tremendous sense of bitterness because the Roman armies occupied Israel. One of the most bitter pills to swallow was the edict that any Roman soldier could require any Jewish male who was at least 12 years of age to carry his military pack or any other burden one mile, but no more. Historically, it was noted that each Jewish male had marked off a mile in each direction from his home so he knew exactly how far to carry this burden.

The first mile was involuntary service…but going the second mile was an investment given voluntarily! Jesus knew that going the second mile was radical living. Each voluntary second or third mile would create love among His followers for the Roman soldiers and open the door for many to become Christians! Radical? Yes! Effective? Absolutely!

But there's more if you're still not convinced. Jesus also taught, "And if someone wants to sue you and take your tunic, let him have your cloak as well" (Matthew 5:40). This principle was so powerful and so important that it was to be carried out whether or not your offender had just or unjust causes against you. The "cloak" was the garment used as protection against the night cold and giving it away represented a sacrificial investment. Jesus knows that if you do not voluntarily invest in the life of the one toward whom you are bitter, toward whom you offer forgiveness, you will never really experience the potential of redemptive love!

Try it! You'll be surprised!

(Matthew 5:40-41; 6:21)

POWER POINT: This week, when someone offends you, return good for evil. In other words, do something nice for them instead of accusing them or taking revenge. When you've done this a few times, you'll begin to understand how God feels and reacts when we offend Him!

Chapter 21

WHAT ABOUT THE FUTURE?

Let's say that you have gone through the process of forgiveness and you've been released from the painful past. What about the future? How do you move into a more controlled future?

Hannah Arendt in her book, *The Human Condition*, wrote: "The only way to overcome the un-predictability of your future is through the power of promising!" Therefore, if forgiving is the only remedy for your painful past, promising is the only remedy for your uncertain future.

A human promise is an awesome reality. When a woman makes a promise, she thrusts her hand into the unpredictable circumstances of her tomorrow and creates a bit of predictable reality. When a man makes a promise, he creates an island of certainty in a rolling, heaving ocean of uncertainty. Is there any other human act, other than forgiving, that is more God-like? Human destiny is resting completely on a promise! Human freedom comes into its own only through a promise! Human community can be saved only through the making and keeping of promises!

The total future of our human family rides on the fragile fibers of a promise spoken long ago! One thing assures us that the cosmos will continue to rotate and not climax its travel through space by turning itself into a stinking garbage heap. One thing affirms that the human romance will have a happy ending and that eventually we will have a new earth populated by a redeemed family! One thing says you can be forgiven and redeemed! The single thread by which everything hangs is a promise spoken and not forgotten!

The awesome One, the eternal One said: "I AM HE WHO WILL BE THERE WITH YOU" (Exodus 3:14, Murray Translation)! Whenever you and I make and keep a promise, we are as close to being like God as we can ever be. (Forgiving, as we have seen, is the other quality that moves us into being like God in action.) A promise is a claim that the person who makes it has the power to act freely to bring order and dependability into an unpredictable future. Whenever we humans make a promise, we are staking a claim on freedom.

Some years ago, Coach Joe Paterno and his Penn State football team were playing for the national championship against Alabama in the Sugar Bowl. They most likely would have won, but they had a touchdown called back because there was a twelfth man on the field. After the game, Paterno was asked to identify the man: "It's only a game," he said. "I have no intention of ever identifying the boy. He just made a mistake." By taking the position of coach, Joe Paterno had promised to support his team members. They knew they could count on him.

When I make a promise, I declare that my future with people is not determined by my inherited chromosomes, nor by the circumstances of my upbringing, nor by the mixed up culture of our times! When this promise is made, I rise above all the conditions that limit me.

No German shepherd ever promised to always stay with me. No home computer ever promised to be forever dependable. Only a person can make a promise; and when we do, we are most free! When you make a promise, you tie yourself to other people by the unseen fibers of loyalty. You agree to commit yourself to someone, come what may. When everything tells them they can count on nothing or no one else, they know they can count on you. You have created a small sanctuary of trust within the chaos of life. All of us, each of us, gets identity from the promises we make and keep.

Do you remember Thomas Moore? Meg, his beautiful daughter, begged him to save his life by renouncing an oath he had once made. All he had to do to save his skin was to break a vow. But to deny a vow is to deny oneself. Listen as he speaks: "When a man takes an oath, Meg, he is holding his own self in his hand, like water. And if he opens his fingers, then he needn't hope to find himself again!"

The people whom I am responsible for, those who depend upon me, also know me by the promises I have made and kept. What I promise is what I am and will be to them.

All humanity...from ghetto to global village depends on the power of promising. Where and when people no longer promise, we are adrift in a sea of uncertainty and confusion.

God is the one who creates for us a new past and a new future by forgiving us and making promises to us. As I am reading the pages of the human experience, I can still see here and there people sharing in God's life to this creative extent: They create a new past for themselves by forgiving people who hurt them, and they create a new future for the forgiven as well as for others by making and keeping promises to people who need them.

(Exodus 3:14, Murray Translation)

⚡ POWER POINT: Forgiving and promising have this in common: they both produce freedom. Forgiving brings freedom from the past, promising brings freedom to the future. Are there promises you have made and not kept? Do you need to ask forgiveness for these lapses? Do you need to renew your promises?

Chapter 22

FORGIVENESS AS A WAY OF LIFE

In the days of our American Revolution, a Baptist minister, Peter Miller, enjoyed the friendship of General George Washington. In the same town in which Miller ministered was a man named Michael Wittman, an evil man who did all in his power to abuse and oppose the minister. During the war, Wittman was involved in treason, arrested, and sentenced to death, the death of a spy. The old preacher walked 70 miles to Philadelphia to plead for the man's life. But Washington said, "No, Peter, I cannot grant you the life of your friend."

Miller exclaimed, "My friend? This is the bitterest enemy I have!"

Washington then inquired, "You've walked 70 miles to save the life of an enemy? That puts the matter in a different light. I will grant the pardon."

The goal is to have forgiveness become your way of life! To think that we needn't forgive until we are asked is a myth that must be exploded. Forgive immediately, even if you are not asked to do so! Forgive continually! Forgive as an intrinsic part of your lifestyle!

Living a forgiving lifestyle is to give wholehearted acceptance to others. This is not a perfect world, and forgiveness is the bumper of life—it protects us from greater harm. There is no genuine forgiveness without genuine acceptance of other people as they are, warts and all. But it's more than a shallow, hollow acceptance; it's more than mere tolerance.

The apostolic writer, Paul, says, "Accept one another, then, just as Christ accepted you, in order to bring praise to God" (Romans 15:7). To do this with a lifestyle is to accept another in a way which gets our sleeves rolled up and our hands dirty in helping, serving, lifting, and changing other lives into the full freedom of forgiveness. This is releasing God's forgiveness as well as yours!

Forgiveness is not leaving a person with the burden of *something* to live down; it's offering that person *someone* to live with—a wonderful, forgiving friend like you! If you choose this kind of a lifestyle, you can be assured that it will be tested. Such tests come as the daily kind of forgiving love which gives and takes, freely accepts the bruises and hurts of living, no matter how difficult the blows of life are dealt to us.

A man lost his oldest son, a fine, clean-cut, brilliant young man. It happened in an auto accident, and a drunk driver was at fault. This father said: "I'm not going to take the quick, easy way of becoming bitter or rebellious about it. My son is gone; someday we will meet again. In the meanwhile, I will be twice the man I would have been. Since he won't be here, I will try to do the work of two men's lives...his and mine." And he's doing it! Turning tragedy to triumph! Through forgiveness, he has drained this tragedy of all its power to destroy another life.

There is an even greater test—living with people and the constant give-and-take of life. The grease of forgiving love will reduce the frictions involved and pour a fresh salve on any irritations. So what if so-and-so rubs you the wrong way? Forgiving love will help you overlook annoyances and even eliminate this type of irritated reaction to others. Nothing is impossible to those who are willing to love! Forgiving love

> *has good manners and does not pursue selfish advantage. It is not touchy. It does not keep account of evil or gloat over the wickedness of other people. On the contrary, it is glad with all good men when truth prevails. Love knows no limit to its endurance, no end to its trust, no fading of its hope; it can outlast anything. It is in fact, the one thing that still stands when all else has fallen"* (I Corinthians 13:5-8, Phillips Translation).

You don't have it? You can! Open your life totally to the life of Christ living in you. As you know Him more clearly, follow Him more nearly, then forgiving love can be yours.

The forgiving kind of lifestyle forgives immediately, forgives continually, and forgives absolutely! It was said of Abraham Lincoln: "His heart had no room for the memory of a wrong."

Forgetting will then follow forgiving! Beyond forgiving and forgetting, there is healing, there is reconciliation! Forgiveness is complete when the severed friendship is restored. A forgiving lifestyle gives love where the enemy expects hate...gives freedom where the enemy deserves punishment...gives understanding where the enemy anticipates revenge. It refuses to seek its own advantage. It gives back to the other person freedom and a new future.

It works for the first time...and it will work for the next 489 times!

(Romans 15:7; I Corinthians 13:5-8)

POWER POINT: The power of forgiving will only be unleashed as you act upon what you have learned about forgiveness. Try implementing some of the suggestions made in this book one at a time and see the difference it makes in your life!